IMAGES
of America

EL PASO AND THE
MEXICAN REVOLUTION

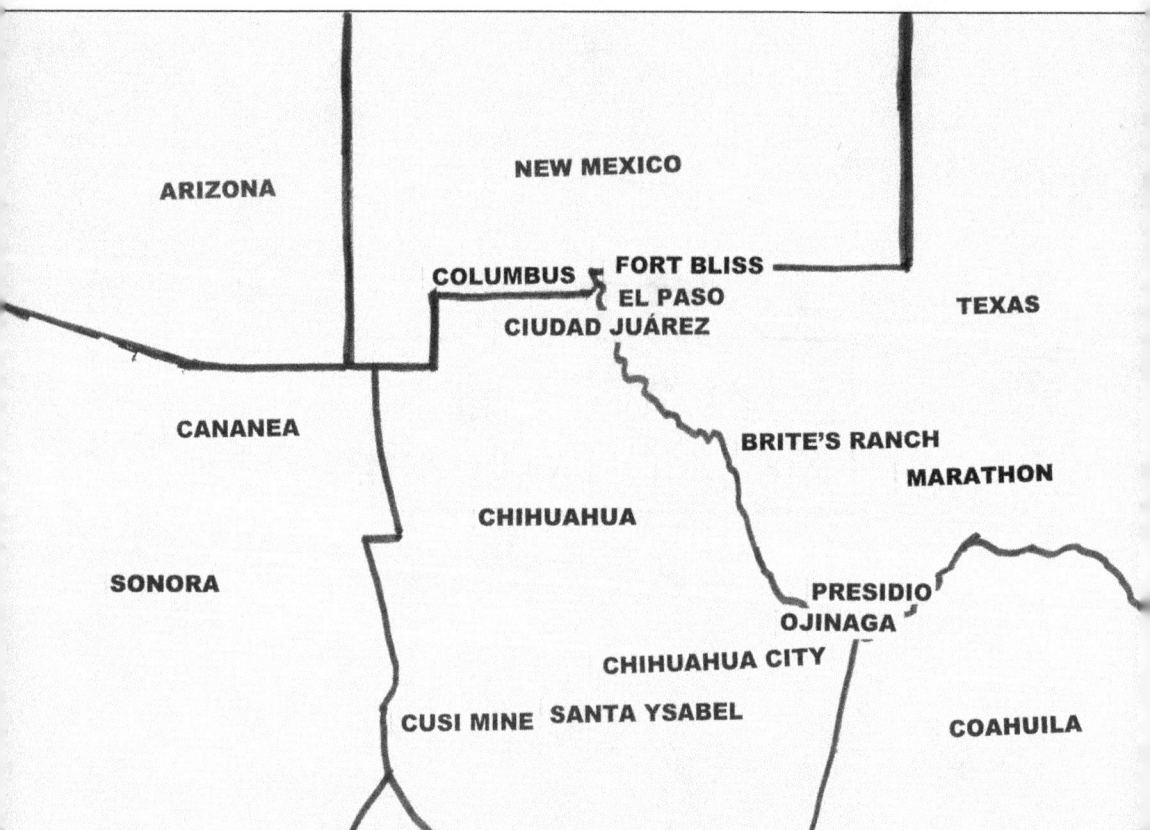

The area covered by this book ranges from the Big Bend of Texas to the boot hill of New Mexico. This map shows only those areas mentioned. (Courtesy of El Paso County Historical Society.)

ON THE COVER: Although the Mexican Revolution was on the south side of the border, El Pasoans were keenly interested in what was going on. This can be seen in the Jim A. Alexander photograph taken from the Mexican side of the Rio Grande. The river separating the United States and Mexico is narrow most of the time. Madero's camp is on the right side of the river. The smelter train carried people from downtown El Paso a distance of 3 miles to a spot immediately across the river from Madero's camp. Both sides are wading in the Rio Grande. The home of the superintendent of the smelter can be seen on the hill. The Mexican Revolution was an immediate presence for the city. There was much curiosity. The postcard is from the El Paso County Historical Society Mexican Revolution collections. (Courtesy of El Paso County Historical Society.)

IMAGES
of America

EL PASO AND THE
MEXICAN REVOLUTION

Patricia Haesly Worthington

ARCADIA
PUBLISHING

Published by Arcadia Publishing
Charleston, South Carolina

Library of Congress Control Number: 2010926992

For all general information, please contact Arcadia Publishing:
Telephone 843-853-2070
Fax 843-853-0044
E-mail sales@arcadiapublishing.com
For customer service and orders:
Toll-Free 1-888-313-2665

Visit us on the Internet at www.arcadiapublishing.com

*This book is dedicated to the C. L. Sonnichsen Special
Collections librarians at The University of Texas at El Paso,
without whom archivists and researchers in El Paso could
not function; to Richard D. Worthington for all his support;
and to the memory of Fannie Mae and Gerson Haesly,
my parents, who always nurtured my interest in history.*

CONTENTS

ACKNOWLEDGMENTS

In the El Paso archival community there are three groups without whom no one can accomplish complete research on El Paso. They are the Special Collections Department at The University of Texas at El Paso (UTEP), the Border Heritage Department at the El Paso Public Library, and the El Paso County Historical Society. Each maintains major collections on varying subjects, especially the Mexican Revolution. I want to thank Claudia Rivers, Laura Hollingsed, Abbie Weiser, and Yvette Delgado (a genius on the computer) in Special Collections at UTEP, who do everything. Marta Estrada, Danny Gonzalez, and Claudia Ramirez in the Border Heritage Department at the El Paso Public Library provided ready access to their very large photographic collections. Richard D. Worthington provided pictures from his collection and tolerated my long hours of attention to this project. From long ago, I also want to thank those people from the original Pioneer Association who made it a point to keep memorabilia from the important events they witnessed. Their efforts are the foundation of the Historical Society's archival collection. It is a joy to work with all that they did.

Unless otherwise indicated, all pictures and scrapbook items are from the archives of the El Paso County Historical Society.

INTRODUCTION

The Mexican Revolution did not happen overnight. An entire series of events occurred before it began. It can be traced to the fall of Maximilian and the ascension of Benito Juárez in 1858. Juárez was a Zapotec Indian who is still revered. He died in 1872 and was succeeded by a member of his government. Soon, however, Porfirio Díaz overthrew the new president. He remained in office until he was overthrown by Mexican revolutionary forces in 1911.

Díaz ruled with an iron fist. He confiscated land and suppressed numerous groups of people, especially including the indigenous Indians. The influence of the upper classes grew to the point that only 2 percent of the population controlled the majority of Mexico's land. For example, Luis Terrazas ruled Chihuahua from a ranch of over 2 million acres. Díaz also worked closely with foreign business interests to develop Mexico's mining industry. Silver had long been mined in central Mexico. The western part of the country yielded copper, in particular, and numerous other metals, including gold. Wealthy foreign industrialists owned and operated the majority of the mines, including such well-known American names as Guggenheim, Hearst, and Palmer. It is widely believed that the actual outbreak of the Mexican Revolution was the strike at the mines at Cananea on the western side of the Sierra Madre.

By 1885, the Mexican Central Railroad reached from the Gulf of Mexico to Ciudad Juárez and across the Rio Grande to the smelter in El Paso. Numerous small railroads developed from remote mines to the mainline routes. The American Smelting and Mining Company (ASARCO), to which ore was directed, became the largest custom smelter in the world. Eleven different railroads provided ore from Mexico, New Mexico, and Arizona. While several routes were completely disrupted by the revolution, ore was still received at the smelter. It did not shut down, and, in actuality, provided the revolutionaries with income since they controlled the incoming ore from Mexico. ASARCO also bought other mines in the United States so that the smelter would have a steady supply of ore.

In 1909, pressure was growing in Mexico for a change in government because of the cruelty of the Díaz dictatorship. The United States became concerned about the growing turmoil because of its numerous business interests in Mexico. Díaz needed a show of foreign support for his regime. Both needed to address the geographical border problem resulting from the periodic flooding of the Rio Grande. This is the Chamizal problem that actually took numerous decades to solve. These concerns resulted in the Taft-Díaz meeting of October 16, 1909.

The Taft-Díaz meeting was significant, but not for business or political reasons. It was the first time that a sitting president of either the United States or Mexico left his country to meet with a foreign head of state. In that respect, it was a glorious meeting, lasting only 11 hours. The meeting was highly scripted. The important topics were covered in two private meetings of no more than 15 minutes each. They did not solve the problems that each sought to discuss. Within just a year, Díaz was deposed and fled to Paris, where he died, and American business interests were sorely tested in the unrest that followed. The Mexican Revolution disrupted international business all along the border. El Paso's business profited greatly from the revolution, however. It was in a perfect geographic position on the border and in a stable country.

For the next 20 years, turmoil and unrest were fairly normal. There were three battles for Juárez—and much intrigue. El Pasoans were keenly interested in all the activity. They observed the revolutionary events and personally knew many of the participants. Many of the revolutionaries lived in the city and certainly used its businesses. At the beginning, the city's citizens supported the *insurrectos*, but as time passed and atrocities worsened, support waned. It changed completely with the massacre at Santa Ysabel and the Columbus raid. At this point, Pancho Villa became an outlaw and was hunted. In Mexico itself, after Díaz was overthrown, three presidents were assassinated and another fled the country.

Since 1848, the post at Fort Bliss has been a major presence in El Paso. It is, without a doubt, the most significant entity in the city today. It was a cavalry and infantry post at the time of the Mexican Revolution, and its commanders and soldiers were very much aware of the problems in Mexico and their nearness to the American border. Everyone was on alert. It housed refugees who were escaping both the battles and persecution. As time and events passed, it became actively involved in the revolution after the raid on Columbus, New Mexico. Gen. John Pershing led the expedition into Mexico to capture Pancho Villa. It did not succeed. However, that incursion brought to the forefront inadequacies in the U.S. Army that were corrected by the time the units left for World War I.

Pancho Villa was assassinated in Parral, Chihuahua, Mexico, in 1923. This was covered widely in El Paso. During the same time, though, the city dealt with interference from the Ku Klux Klan that had gained control of the school board but was stopped in 1924 by the efforts of a brave lawyer. Life was returning to normal until Gen. José Gonzalo Escobar attempted another revolution in 1929. This was a strange revolution that did not succeed. Escobar fled Mexico to the United States, taking with him a large sum of money that Mexico sued to regain.

Much myth and lore has followed the Mexican Revolution of 1911. Pancho Villa is a hero to some and a villain to others. The activities of this revolutionary period and all its participants provided El Paso, Texas, a colorful history. At the same time, the city continued to grow normally; new businesses opened, others expanded, and the city itself grew significantly, with some of that population being refugees from Mexico.

One

EL PASO

THE INTERNATIONAL CITY

The five Cs—cotton, copper, cattle, climate, and clothes—were the main words describing El Paso's growth. One very important factor, however, is geographic location. The city's position on the border, divided by an usually narrow river, brought a unique set of circumstances. For centuries the population was on the south side of the Rio Grande. Spanish missions and missionaries began arriving in the 1500s. Settlements developed on the north side of the river, with names such as Fabens, Concordia, Franklin, and then El Paso. Fort Bliss was founded in 1848; Anson Mills platted the city in 1859. The Civil War and Salt War (1876) disrupted land titles and peace. In 1878, the county seat was moved from Ysleta to El Paso. With the arrival of the railroad in 1881, modern El Paso grew quickly. El Paso was, and still is, a good weather crossroads for travel.

The railroads provided business and growth. At one time, more than 11 rail lines came into the city. The bulk of traffic came from the mines of Mexico, New Mexico, and Arizona. The American Mining and Smelting Company (1887) was the largest custom smelter in the world, yet it was but one of four smelters in the city. Its plant was on the north bank of the Rio Grande. The sandy banks of Mexico were an estimated 25 feet across, more during a flood. The International Bridge (pedestrian and rail) was freely traversed, just as the river had been for centuries, and there was a footbridge. The city had commerce, banks, restaurants, hotels, and a famous red-light district. It grew constantly and was a mecca for all sorts of activities.

For example, between 1900 and 1910, there were many activities concentrated in the southern part of the city near the Rio Grande in Chihuahuita and El Segundo Barrio. Numerous Spanish-language newspapers were printed, and several political activists operated. One of the best known was Teresita Urrea, also dubbed "The Saint of Cabora." She had a strong local following and was sought by Mexican federal agents. Another well-known activist was Ricardo Flores Magón, who had great influence in Mexico and was also sought by Díaz's agents. There was such intense opposition to Díaz that the United States feared for the presidents' safety during their visit in 1909, especially on the drive through south El Paso.

Fred Feldman photographed the flood of May 1897 from the roof of the county courthouse. Notice of the pending flood appeared in the El Paso newspapers for about a week prior to its arrival. Still, proper precautions were not taken, and great destruction resulted. This flood changed El Paso's history and emphasized the Chamizal problems by changing the course of the Rio Grande once again.

Simeon Hart's mill was on the river and survived numerous floods. It was opened early in the 19th century. Some of its buildings are still standing and used for commercial purposes. Fort Bliss was once located at this site.

The Southern Pacific Railroad arrived in 1881, followed closely by the Atchison, Topeka, and Santa Fe Railroad and the Texas Pacific Railroad. The rail yards for the Southern Pacific Railroad are shown in this 1907 Francis Parker panorama. A strip north of the rail yard and Union Depot is now U.S. Interstate 10. The Texas Pacific route through El Paso skirted the river south of town and then joined the main line west of the city.

The Southern Pacific Railroad bridges (now Union Pacific) crossed the Rio Grande immediately north of the smelter. Several smaller lines brought ore from Arizona, New Mexico, and Mexico to the smelter for processing. These bridges are busy even today. They were protected by troops during the Mexican Revolution. The El Paso Brick Plant is in the foreground.

11

Juarez, Mexico from El Paso – May 3, 1914

The International Bridge had customs houses at both ends. However, it was easy to cross back and forth until the outbreak of World War I. In this picture, the United States is on the right. The only international streetcar in the world is getting ready to cross into Mexico. The Mexican Central Railroad Bridge (the Black Bridge) is the second bridge. During the Mexican Revolution, a company of military was camped on the sandy area adjacent to the American Customs House.

The American Mining and Smelting Company (ASARCO) was adjacent to the Rio Grande 3 miles from downtown. The smelter train ran from town to the plant. Note the footbridge crossing the river. Madero's camp was very close to the international boundary marker. He used the footbridge to return to the United States at night, where he stayed in a house nearby. The footbridge no longer exists.

El Paso was a fast-growing metropolis. This view looks south and includes City Hall, the original county courthouse, and Everybody's department store. Beyond the county courthouse to the river is El Segundo Barrio. Can you spot the elephant?

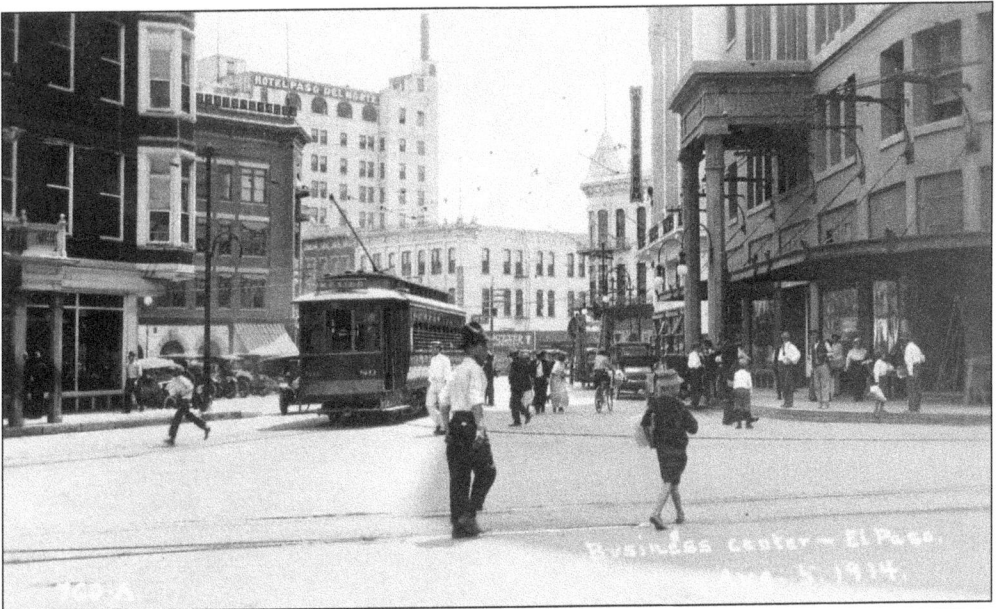

In 1914, the business district was bustling. El Paso had a growth spurt of building in 1906. With the railroads, mining, and Fort Bliss continually growing, keeping up with progress was important. This is the intersection looking east through Pioneer Plaza, an area that is still busy.

El Segundo Barrio and Chihuahuita are the south El Paso neighborhoods closest to the river and the Santa Fe street bridge leading to Mexico. Houses were close. They were areas where one could hide, and numerous people with revolutionary aims did just that. One could also be shot during

a battle if he were adjacent to the river. These facts caused great concern during the Taft-Díaz visit. The areas were hit hard by the flu epidemic of 1918.

San Antonio Street is one of El Paso's oldest. It was on the original 1859 plat of the city. On the right in this view is the First National Bank; then we see the Wigwam Saloon. After it is the original location of the State National Bank. On the left is the Parlor Bar and Mickleson's cigar store. About two blocks down on the left was the Acme Saloon, where John Wesley Hardin was shot.

The Caples building is at one of the busiest intersections in downtown El Paso, the southeast corner of Mesa and San Antonio Streets. Both Pancho Villa and Pascual Orozco had offices in the building. Originally designed and built by noted architect Henry Trost, today the building is on the Texas list of the 10 most endangered historic buildings in the state.

Revolutionaries were short on supplies, ammunition, and guns. Many downtown businesses provided varying kinds of support to revolutionaries and citizens alike. The Krakauer, Zork, and Moye business was among those that sold large amounts of arms and ammunition to the *insurrectos*. Sheldon Payne Arms, Momsen-Dunnagan-Ryan, and other small companies also participated in arms sales. Pancho Villa loved ice cream at the Elite Confectionary, and all groups shopped at the Popular Dry Goods Company. Needless to say, the many saloons in El Paso and Juárez were frequented. All businesses profited greatly from revolutionary activities. (Courtesy Otis A. Aultman Collection, Border Heritage Department, El Paso Public Library.)

The Schwartz family founded the Popular Dry Goods Company. It served generations of El Pasoans since before 1900.

The Toltec building still stands. It is across from the county courthouse and originally housed an elegant gentlemen's club. Several prominent *insurrectos* were guests at one time. Today it is an endangered structure.

The Sheldon Hotel that faced El Paso's Little Plaza was the preferred place of residence for both *insurrectos* and the press. Pres. William Howard Taft rested here during his visit. It burned down in 1929.

This interior shot of the Parlor Bar provides a look at a business whose taxes helped support the city during its early years. The houses of prostitution also provided significant tax dollars. Saloons closed or moved to Juárez during Prohibition, and the bordellos officially closed in 1937. Both prospered during the Mexican Revolution.

Numerous businesses continued to function and provide services to the city during the revolution. The Texas Company operated in South El Paso near the railroads.

The El Paso Dairy Company was one of the first in the city. It was the forerunner of several successful dairies.

One of the first housing additions north of downtown El Paso was developed by J. Fisher Satterthwaite. Today it is know as Sunset Heights. The division sits on hills overlooking downtown and the river. Pancho Villa and Victoriano Huerta were among the revolutionary leaders who lived in the area. Residents sat on their balconies and watched the battles in Juárez. This is the 510 Prospect residence of Pancho Villa. Huerta's house was destroyed long ago.

The Ernst Kohlberg house is a Henry Trost design and is located in Sunset Heights. The family sat on the upstairs balcony and watched the Battle of Juárez.

In the early 20th century, people from all over the United States came to El Paso at their doctors' recommendations because they had tuberculosis. It was thought that the city's dry climate would help with the healing process. One of the most famous of the sanitoriums was the Hendricks-Laws Sanitorium. Dr. C. M. Hendricks was in charge. He also was active in civic affairs and is credited with naming the Sun Bowl and serving as its president for numerous years.

The Albert Baldwin Sanatorium, El Paso, Texas.

All the tuberculosis sanatoriums were located on the eastern side of the Franklin Mountains. At the time, that was the center of town and also in the cooler mountain air. The Albert Baldwin Sanatorium was one of the first built. Baldwin sold his interest to Dr. R. Homan. Over the years, this sanatorium eventually became Southwestern General Hospital.

Dr. Ira Bush had a hospital for wounded insurrectionists on South Campbell Street. The building does not exist today. Dr. Bush went into the thick of battle in order to help both federal troops and insurrectionists. Pictured is his El Paso home. It was built after the revolution.

El Paso's summer heat and, at that time, frontier conditions caused many problems among the city's babies. At one time the city had the highest infant death rate in the country. To alleviate the problem, a baby sanitarium was built in the mountains at Cloudcroft, New Mexico. Each summer a train took the babies to the mountains to wait out the summer heat, returning in the fall.

Numerous new undertakings transpired while revolution prevailed in Mexico. One of the important ones was the founding of the Texas College of Mines in 1914. It specialized in engineering and geology due to the prevalence of mining in the area. The college opened in vacated buildings at Fort Bliss but was given land by ASARCO within a few years, at which time it began the campus that is known today as The University of Texas at El Paso.

The El Paso Rubber Company was advertising road maps to the west. However, the roads might be plank at this time.

El Paso High School is the city's oldest, but its original building no longer stands. Before 1916, it received a visit from Charles Evans Hughes and William Jennings Bryan. In 1916, the new El Paso High School opened. Designed by Henry Trost, the building is still an active high school.

The El Paso School for Girls was founded in 1910 in two houses in Sunset Heights. It has since become known as Radford School, and its campus moved to the eastern side of El Paso. One of its well-known graduates is retired Supreme Court Justice Sandra Day O'Connor.

Cathedral High School opened in 1929. It is a male-only school that boasts a 100-percent college matriculation rate since its opening. It is attached to St. Patrick's Cathedral.

One of the biggest construction projects began in 1910 and resulted in the building of Elephant Butte Dam near Truth or Consequences, New Mexico. It was completed in 1916 and is about 100 miles north of El Paso. The dam, one of the largest concrete dams in the world, addressed the centuries' old problem of the wandering path of the Rio Grande, the source of the Chamizal disagreements. Today Caballo Dam, that is downstream, aids in river regulation.

Long-standing organizations, such as the Woman's Club of El Paso, built new headquarters during the revolutionary period. The oldest woman's club in the state of Texas also has the distinction of having the first free-standing woman's club building in the state. This structure is an official historic building, as designated by the National Trust for Historic Preservation. In its early days, the club's members were very active in the development of the city and helped roll bandages and care for victims of the Mexican Revolution.

The El Paso Country Club opened near Washington Park in 1906. In 1909, it moved to northeast El Paso, where a clubhouse was constructed. The club used the building for seven years before it was destroyed by fire, at which time it moved to the Upper Valley, near the Rio Grande.

One of the most significant structures that opened during the revolution was St. Patrick's Cathedral, which was dedicated in 1917. The cathedral and El Paso's large Catholic population warranted a bishop being stationed in the city. Several years ago, the spire was struck by lightning.

Two new businesses that influenced El Paso for several decades were opened during this significant 20-year period. Farah Manufacturing, Inc., began on Leon Street. It became the largest producer of men's slacks in the world.

The second was El Paso Natural Gas. The oil and gas industry was growing, with major discoveries in West Texas. El Paso Natural Gas Company opened its pipeline operation in 1929, when it transported gas from Jal, Texas, into El Paso. The company grew over the years and had its headquarters in downtown El Paso. It has now moved to Houston, Texas, and is known as the El Paso Company.

El Paso's original county courthouse was razed and a new one designed in 1915. It is a Trost and Trost plan. It has changed in appearance today, but the basic structure remains. Originally Liberty Hall was behind the courthouse. It was the center of numerous types of entertainment performances for decades.

Henry Trost was the most significant architect in El Paso's early history. He designed the Mills Building for Anson Mills. It is one of the first concrete structures in the country and is on the site of the old Grand Central Hotel. It has always been an office building and is being renovated to that status today.

In the building boom after 1906, Trost was responsible for many of El Paso's historic buildings. While some have been lost over the years, quite a few remain. Among them are the Scottish Rite Cathedral that is still in full use. The R. E. McKee Company built many of Trost's designs, including this cathedral. McKee's company also began during the revolutionary period and went on to build on the international level.

The Paso del Norte Hotel was designed in 1906 and completed in 1912, just after the Battle of Juárez. Today it is known as the Camino Real.

El Paso's Carnegie Library opened in 1904. It grew under the guidance of especially good librarians, such as Maud Sullivan. This building has been replaced, but the Border Heritage collection remains. The bandstand no longer exists.

El Paso's residential district was growing. Many of the houses depicted in this photograph remain today. Several groups of them are parts of historic districts.

Trinity Methodist Church was one of the first in El Paso, dating back to 1882. In 1906, the structure was built that remains today.

Providence Hospital began in a large house on Santa Fe Street. Its founder was one of the original doctors at the smelter. Today that location is part of Interstate 10. The Providence Hospital complex has moved up the hill. The other big hospital at the time of the revolution was Hotel Dieu, operated by the Daughters of Charity.

Charles Hamilton was the first ever to fly into El Paso in 1910. He landed in Washington Park, where Jim Alexander took this photograph.

IN HONOR OF
COLONEL CHARLES A. LINDBERGH
SEPTEMBER TWENTY-FOURTH
1927
EL PASO

Charles Lindbergh was in El Paso for about two hours in 1927 during the national tour of the *Spirit of St. Louis*. This is a copy of the cover of the program. A tipica orchestra played and Mexican songs were sung; Elizabeth Garrett (Pat Garrett's daughter) sang a medley of western songs, perhaps written by her. Mayor R. E. Thomason introduced all the guests. The event's program concluded with an address by Col. Charles A. Lindbergh, who presented a gift to the city. Lunch was served. Excerpts from Lindbergh's "We" were the last page of the program.

Overlooking the entire area are the Franklin Mountains that run through the middle of the city and divide the east side from the west side. They are a state park and, as such, are the largest state park within a city's boundaries in the United States. At one time they had the only tin mine that existed in the country. It was not successful.

Over the 20 years of Mexican Revolution, life went on as normal in El Paso. In Mexico, however, conditions were quite different. There was great disparity between the rich and the very poor. While American business flourished, particularly in mining, the conditions under which the workers functioned were sometimes primitive. At one time, Indians working in the mines carried the ore on their backs. This picture is from the Parral area, as shown in the *Transactions of the American Institute of Mining Engineers*, Mexican Meeting, volume XXXII, 1902.

Two

THE TAFT-DÍAZ MEETING AND THE BEGINNING OF REVOLUTION

William Howard Taft became the U.S. president in March 1909. He did not really want the job and was very sensitive to criticism, a fact that became especially troublesome when Congress enacted the highest tariff in the history of the country. In Mexico, Porfirio Díaz directed a dictatorship with widespread unrest developing. Even though he was in his 80s, he wanted to continue his rule. Mayor Joseph Sweeney of El Paso, among others, corresponded with both presidents to arrange a meeting between them. It happened October 16, 1909. Taft was seeking protection for American business interests in Mexico, and Díaz wanted American support for his regime and for attention to be paid to the Chamizal problem.

The Rio Grande is not a large river, but when it flooded, it meandered wildly. The border's shape has changed on numerous occasions. Official records that began in 1850 with the Emory Survey show the course of the river at the base of the Franklin Mountains. The channel pushed farther south over the decades. Then, it would shift north for a while. Bancos were created that both countries claimed. The massive flood of 1897 changed many boundaries and caused much damage but sparked diplomatic negotiations to solve the periodic flooding problems. The settlement of this matter was the Chamizal Agreement of 1964, when the river was channeled through El Paso.

At the same time, massive unrest developed in Mexico over the Díaz dictatorship. El Paso was used as a safe place, a supply source, and a bank for *insurrectos* who were trying to overthrow the Mexican government. El Paso remained a center of activity during the next 20 years of Mexican Revolution. There was much activity to the point that El Paso Mayor Joseph Sweeney warned the Department of State about dangerous areas of the city. The merchants were quite happy with the lucrative business, although several were challenged by the U. S. government for making illegal sales.

In order to discuss the situation in each country, U.S. president William Howard Taft and Mexican president Porfirio Díaz met in El Paso on October 16, 1909. It was a one-day visit that was historically significant. For each, it was the first time that a sitting president had left his country to meet with a foreign head of state on foreign soil. Fred Feldman took this official portrait at the *Aduana* (Customs House) in Juárez.

The federal building that also housed the post office was decorated grandly for the presidential visits. The leaders of El Paso requested federal help to pay for decorations but were told that the government did not support such events. El Paso formed a committee of prominent citizens who orchestrated everything.

Union Depot was also decorated, as was every building of significance in El Paso, especially the offices of the El Paso and Southwestern Railroad, the Orndorff Hotel, and the El Paso Herald Post. Noted photographer Fred Feldman was the chairman of the decorations committee. This structure was designed by noted architect Daniel Burnham.

The Orndorff Hotel looked particularly beautiful with the flags draping its balconies and columns. Dr. Ira Bush, who set up a hospital to treat those injured while fighting, lived here during revolutionary years.

The El Paso and Southwestern building represented well the region's transportation interests. Their line, in particular, carried much ore from western mines to the smelter in El Paso.

President Taft arrived in El Paso from Albuquerque. He was feted at the St. Regis Hotel just south of the railroad tracks. His personal railroad car "the Mayflower" was parked exactly across Oregon Street. Taft had only a short distance to walk. (Courtesy of Otis A. Aultman Collection, Border Heritage Department, El Paso Public Library.)

The St. Regis Hotel was one of El Paso's oldest but most elegant hotels in the city. Breakfast was served to Taft and invited guests—men only. Favors from the breakfast are highly sought collectibles today and include such items as badges and engraved silver matchboxes.

The official party met President Taft as he left the train. All were told to wear morning coats and top hats. Taft was then escorted into the St. Regis for breakfast, though he had already eaten grandly on his train. (Courtesy of Otis A. Aultman Collection, Border Heritage Department, El Paso Public Library.)

From the hotel, Taft was driven to the El Paso Chamber of Commerce, where he was joined by Porfirio Díaz for a meeting. Díaz arrived by carriage. The exterior of the building was decorated like the rest of El Paso. Their short meeting was not recorded.

Taft and Díaz met in the main chamber hall that was properly decorated for such a meeting. However, Taft's excessive weight caused the chair in which he was sitting to break. The chair was saved but has disappeared over the years.

After the meeting at the Chamber of Commerce, President Taft went to Juárez to continue the meeting with Díaz. Upon returning to El Paso, Taft joined one of the grandest parades the city ever had. Dr. Hugh Stevenson planned the event and was its grand marshall. He also kept an excellent scrapbook of the visit.

President Taft rode the route through the city in an automobile rather than the horse-drawn carriage that was used for the formal meetings with Díaz. He covered the whole route before reaching the reviewing stand. The parade-reviewing stand was in Cleveland Square across from the St. Regis Hotel. It is the site of the El Paso Museum of History today.

The cadets from the El Paso Military Institute were among the many military units that marched in the parade. Following the parade, Taft rested before going to Juárez and an official state dinner. (Jim Alexander photograph.)

President Taft crossed the Rio Grande in a carriage to the *Aduana*. The building and the route to it were elaborately decorated to fit the occasion. Here Mexican soldiers in full dress uniform line the International Bridge.

The *Aduana* was equally festooned. Official photographs were taken before the participants sat down for dinner. Toasts were made. The exact dialogue for the toasts went through many weeks of editing at the State Department. No detail was left to chance.

This is the only known picture taken of the dining room at the *Aduana* on October 16, 1909. By train from Mexico City, Porfirio Díaz brought Maximilian's china and cut glass from Chapultepec Castle. The two sets were valued at well over $1 million. To date, a search has not located any remaining pieces of this service.

Following dinner, Taft left Mexico, where the columns that had been placed for decoration were bathed in electric lights, and returned to the Mayflower. He then departed El Paso after less than a 12-hour visit. (Courtesy Otis A. Aultman Collection, Border Heritage Department, El Paso Public Library.)

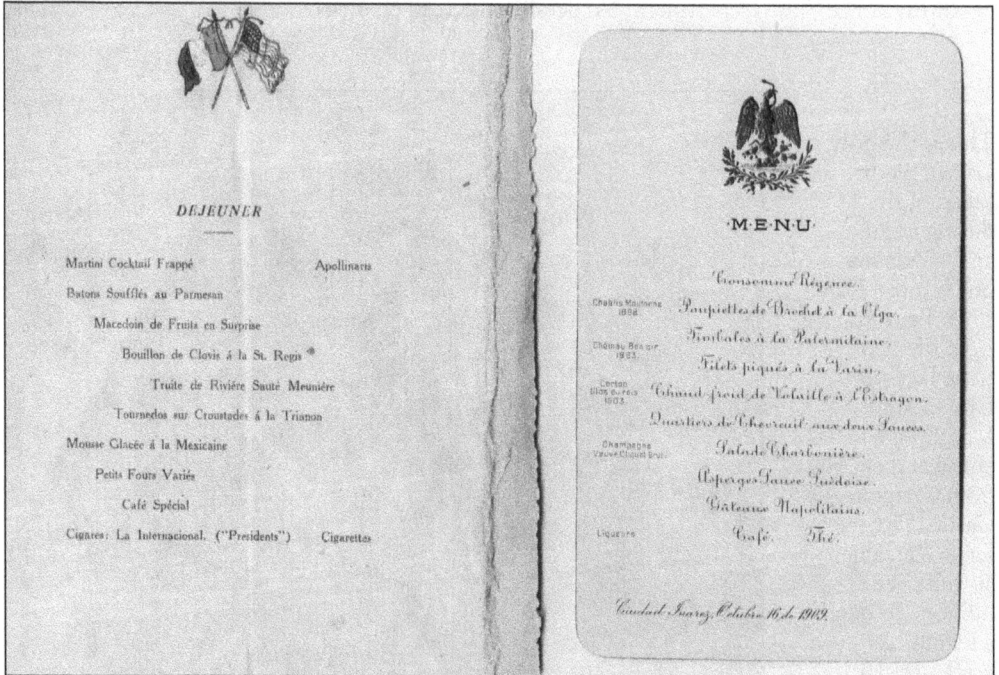

The breakfast and dinner menus were both in French. The meals were elaborate, and El Paso imported its waiters from California for the occasion. Mexico also had special service at the *Adauna*.

Three

A Myriad of
Participants

One could not begin to cover all the participants in the Mexican Revolution. All parts of Mexico were involved. In El Paso, businessmen, citizens, and seekers of adventure participated. Soldiers and their commanders from Fort Bliss were also involved.

The revolution began slowly, with Francisco Madero challenging Porfirio Díaz in the presidential election of 1910. Madero began by writing *The Presidential Succession of 1910*, a book that had enormous impact. He formed the Anti-Re-electionist Party to challenge Díaz. He was greeted with enthusiasm while on speaking tours, a fact that alarmed Díaz, who resorted to repressive measures that ended with Madero being imprisoned until the election was over. Díaz was declared the winner, and Madero realized that the only way to change the government was by revolution. He issued "The Plan of San Luis Potosí" that declared the election void and named himself as provisional president. The revolution officially began November 20, 1910.

The beginning did not go well. Madero fled to Texas when his supplies did not arrive and began to reorganize. He faced financial and manpower problems that were soon resolved with the success of manpower recruitment in the Mexican states of Chihuahua and Sonora, in particular. Much support came from the oppressed people of the agricultural and mining areas of Mexico. They were short on guns and ammunition, but from that grew the value of El Paso.

Porfirio Díaz (1830–1915) was a mestizo from the Mexican state of Oaxaca. He pursued the priesthood but joined the army when the Mexican War broke out. He had an illustrious career. He initially supported Benito Juárez but began to disagree with his policies. After Juárez's death, Díaz overthrew the new president and remained in power until 1911. His harsh policies—confiscating land, favoring the upper classes, and attacking the Indians—were the main causes of the Mexican Revolution. He also gave much preferential treatment to foreign companies working in Mexico. After he was overthrown, he fled to Paris, where he died and was buried.

Francisco I. Madero González (1873–1913) was a member of a wealthy family in Coahuila, Mexico. He was well educated at home and abroad. Around 1903, he became politically active. When Díaz announced free elections in 1910, Madero sought the office but was not successful. Díaz chose to remain in office. On November 20, 1910, Madero declared revolution and named himself as provisional president. He left Mexico and eventually traveled to El Paso, where after the first battle of Juárez, he became Mexico's president until his assassination in 1913. (Courtesy of the Stout-Feldman Studio Photographs, PH074, C. L. Sonnichsen Special Collections Department, Library, The University of Texas at El Paso.)

Francisco "Pancho" Villa (1877–1923) was originally named Doroteo Arango and was a native of Durango, Mexico. He returned to a life of crime before joining Madero's revolt in 1910. He frequented both sides of the border and, at one time, lived at 510 Prospect in El Paso. Villa did not drink and was particularly fond of ice cream. However, he was also a very cruel person. He led several successful battles during the revolution. Among them was the Columbus Raid of 1916 that drew the United States (Pershing Expedition) into the Mexican Revolution. He was assassinated in 1923.

Pascual Orozco Jr. (1882–1915) was born in Guerrero, Mexico, and became a successful businessman. He began supporting Madero early in Madero's revolutionary career. Orozco helped buy arms in the United States. He, along with many others, crossed the border freely and frequently. He became a brigadier general in the revolutionary forces but became unhappy and led a revolt of his own against Madero. His only supporter was Victoriano Huerta. The two were to travel in the United States to gain support, but they were arrested north of El Paso. Orozco escaped and fled to the Quitman Mountains with a small group. A posse discovered and killed them. Orozco was buried in El Paso. His body was later returned to Mexico.

Victoriano Huerta (1854–1916) was from Jalisco, Mexico, where he pursued a career in the Mexican military, specializing in cartography. He too reached the rank of brigadier general. Díaz sent him on numerous deployments to suppress uprisings. After Madero declared revolution, Huerta joined the revolutionary forces. He was in and out of favor and had a great ego. He was involved in the execution of Madero that caused a negative reaction in the United States. He fled Mexico in 1914 but sought support for a return to Mexico. He supported Orozco's revolution and was captured with Orozco. Huerta was tried for inciting illegal activity. His lawyer was Tom Lea Jr. He was ordered to remain under house arrest at 415 W. Boulevard (now Yandell). Not too much later, Huerta died of cirrhosis and was buried in Evergreen Cemetery, where he remains today. Mexico considers him to have been a traitor.

Venustiano Carranza (1859–1920) and his family were natives of Coahuila and were supporters of Benito Juárez. He entered politics during the Díaz regime and became disillusioned with him. The ranchers of Coahuila actively opposed some of Díaz's policies regarding their state. Díaz sent a representative to deal with the problem. He and Carranza became friends. Political intrigue forced him to leave Mexico and join Madero in San Antonio. He failed at his initial attempt at revolution and joined Madero in Juárez, where he was named the minister of war. He became governor of Coahuila but rebelled against Huerta when Madero was assassinated. He issued the Plan of Guadalupe that promised a return to constitutional government. He was elected president and recognized by the United States. Two of his most significant accomplishments were the Laws of Reform and a new constitution that still exists. Carranza chose not to run for president again in 1920, but revolutionary forces still existed. He had to flee and was assassinated during his flight.

Giuseppe Garibaldi II (1879–1950) was the grandson of the Garibaldi who unified Italy. He was born in Australia and participated in the Boer War in South Africa. Along with others from that conflict, Garibaldi came to Mexico and served during the beginning of the Mexican Revolution. He set up the medical assistance that would be needed during the battle. He was at the Battle of Juárez and is in many of the pictures of that conflict. However, Villa kicked him out of the army. He returned to Europe where he participated in the first Balkan War and World War I. A plaza in Mexico City is named in his honor. In this photograph, Garibaldi is on the left. An unidentified reporter is on the right.

Emiliano Zapata (1879–1919) was born in Mexico's southern state of Morelos. He was from a large family and had a limited education. He was drafted into the Mexican army but moved to a cavalry position because of his ability with horses. He became involved in politics at the village level and particularly supported agrarian reform. He did not approve of Madero's land plan, and they parted ways very early in the revolution, with Zapata fleeing to the mountains of Puebla. He participated in forming Mexico's most radical reform plan, the Plan de Ayala. Military conflict resulted. Zapata became the rebel leader in southern Mexico, challenging Madero's rule. He refused to disarm and continued his activities for several years. In a ruse, President Carranza arranged an infiltration of Zapata's camp. Zapata was assassinated April 10, 1919. To this day, the southern area of Mexico is a haven for rebel forces seeking basic reforms. Zapata is seated to the left of Pancho Villa, who is in the center of the front row. (Courtesy of the Mexican Revolution Collection, C. L. Sonnichsen Special Collections Department, Library, The University of Texas at El Paso.)

Pictured at the front of this group, Álvaro Obregón (1880–1928) was from the state of Sonora and was a successful chickpea farmer. He was also involved in local government. He joined the military in 1912 as a Madero supporter and developed considerable military skills. After Madero's assassination, Obregón opposed Huerta and supported Carranza, who appointed him commander in chief of northwestern Mexico. He lost an arm in one of the battles. He opposed Carranza's actions in the presidential campaign of 1920 that resulted in Carranza's assassination. Obregón won the election that followed and presided over the most stable government in Mexico since the revolution began. He was in office until 1928, when he won reelection but was opposed and also assassinated.

General of the Armies John J. Pershing (1860–1948) was born in Missouri and attended local schools before being appointed to the U.S. Military Academy in 1878. He participated in the Indian Wars and the Spanish-American War, where he commanded the 10th Cavalry. On returning, he married and spent time in Asia. Pres. Theodore Roosevelt appointed him brigadier general over numerous others. It caused some problems. In 1914, he was appointed to command the Army 8th Cavalry Regiment at Fort Bliss, where he was responsible for security along the U.S.-Mexico border. After the Columbus Raid, he led the Punitive Expedition that failed. The expedition did bring attention to problems with military readiness, however. After the Punitive Expedition, he went to World War I, where he had more distinguished service that resulted in him being named general of the armies, the only person to hold that title except for George Washington. (Courtesy of the Stout-Feldman Studio Photographs, PH075, C. L. Sonnichsen Special Collections Department, Library, The University of Texas at El Paso.)

The relationship between El Pasoans, *insurrectos*, foreign diplomats, and families was common. In this picture Adolph Schwartz (founder of the Popular Dry Goods Company) is on the lower left side; the tall gentleman in the back is German Consul Max Weber. In front is Francisco Madero, standing with his family. Schwartz was approached by Pancho Villa early in the revolution and asked for a loan. Schwartz refused, saying that he did not want to take sides. Villa persisted and told Schwartz that he would be reimbursed. Schwartz finally agreed. Several weeks later, Villa told Schwartz to go to the ore train that had just arrived and cut out the amount of silver that would repay the loan. (Stout-Feldman Studio Photographs, PH075, C. L. Sonnichsen Special Collections Department, Library, The University of Texas at El Paso.)

Four

THE FIRST
BATTLE OF JUÁREZ
MAY 8–11, 1911

The first Battle of Juárez was the largest of the Mexican Revolution. It was covered extensively by local and national media and by many local citizens. Thousands of photographs remain, mostly in the form of postcards.

Lucy Edwards, wife of the American consul in Juárez, reported that the battle was begun by a few *insurrectos* of Madero's army that was camped on the banks of the Rio Grande across from ASARCO. There were men from the Mexican military who did not like Díaz, agricultural and mining workers who had been mistreated, indigenous Indians who had suffered, women (*soldadas*), and American as well as foreign soldiers of fortune. All supported Madero in this initial effort to depose Díaz.

Scouts went back and forth across the river, familiarizing themselves with defenses. Funds were raised, and arms and ammunition purchased. One person remembered her father taking her across the river to Madero's camp, where she sat on Madero's knee, and he pulled her pigtails. The battle affected El Paso, as stray bullets crossed the river and killed several people.

Media from all over the country focused on El Paso. A number of them, as well as some of the soldiers of fortune, made their way to Otis Aultman's studio. The Adventurer's Club was born. Some of its members made lasting names for themselves.

The battle for Juárez began at 8:30 a.m. on March 8, 1911. It lasted four days. According to Lucy Edwards, firing was intense. The consul's residence became a safe haven. All stayed away from the windows and doors. The adobe structure protected them from stray bullets. Eventually the consulate became full of refugees, and Edwards was greatly aided in helping the refugees by two of the Chinese who had survived the Boxer Rebellion. There was much death and destruction all around. Those in the consulate helped people caught in the rebellion escape across the river to safety in El Paso. They could not help the Chinese, however, because of the Chinese Exclusion Act then in force in the United States.

The *insurrectos* won the battle; Díaz was forced to resign. Madero became president of Mexico. There were second and third battles for the city in 1913 and 1919. Its participants were told to attack solely from the east and west so that no bullets would fall on the United States.

In 1911, the bridge across the Rio Grande was level. The boundary between the United States and Mexico is in the middle so that there are entry offices at both ends. This view looks toward El Paso from Juárez.

Mexican officers and guards manned their posts as they posed for this picture.

As tensions mounted in Mexico, the federal forces in Juárez prepared defenses. Barricades were set up along major streets and neighborhoods.

Fort Hidalgo was south of Juárez proper. It was the base for the federal military and was repeatedly attacked by Pancho Villa over a period of several years during the revolution.

This is the international boundary marker, denoting the spot where Texas, New Mexico, and Mexico meet. It is on the west side of the Rio Grande. (Courtesy of the Border Heritage Department, El Paso Public Library.)

The same boundary marker is shown in this 1911 photograph of Madero's camp. Obviously the proximity to the United States is very close. The border was much more casual than it is today. (Courtesy of the Mexican Revolution Collection PH015, C. L. Sonnichsen Special Collections Department, Library, The University of Texas at El Paso.)

Madero's camp stretched into the hills on the west side of the Rio Grande. It would have encompassed what is known today as Mount Cristo Rey. ASARCO's smelter was just across the river.

In this view, Madero's camp is just below the boundary marker that is in the center of the picture. Above the marker are the El Paso Brick Company and the bridges across the Rio Grande.

4/29 1911

Madero's camp was a busy place and one of which many pictures were taken, probably because it was in such easy camera range. At one time, there was a footbridge that crossed the Rio Grande at the site of the smelter. People used it frequently, including Madero, who crossed each night in order to sleep in a house on the smelter grounds. This footbridge no longer exists.

Pascual Orozco's encampment was near that of Madero and also in the Juárez Mountains. It too was stretched out and overlooked the city. It was easy to go through the mountains and attack the city, even by surprise, because of the numerous ravines in the area.

Thousands of Pancho Villa recruitment posters were made and posted in El Paso. While numerous soldiers of fortune joined Villa, it is not known how many citizens of El Paso actually joined the *insurrectos* in their fight.

While Madero and Orozco had camps on the outskirts of the city, Villa's forces came to Juárez by train. Hundreds came from the mountains of Mexico, primarily on the Mexico Northwestern RR.

Villa's troops also marched to the city from areas that had no trains. Long columns of troops and their supporters filed into camps near the city, primarily on its south side.

This card portrays a typical Villista. A Villista was a soldier who supported Pancho Villa's forces in the Mexican Revolution.

Typical Villista.

820.
W.H. Horne
El Paso. Tex

The Sentinel

Over the years, Díaz antagonized the majority of Mexico's native population. When revolution came, these Indians supported the *insurrectos*. This is possibly a staged photograph, but this Indian was serving as a sentinel for revolutionary forces.

Yaqui Indians (sitting) in Madero's camp pose for the photographer. Others stand behind.

Some Indians came to the battle with primitive weapons, such as this bow and arrow. (Courtesy of the C. L. Sonnichsen Special Collections Department, Library, The University of Texas at El Paso.)

Gen. Lucio Blanco and his staff were also in Madero's camp.

Villa conferred with General Ortega. Ortega is walking on Villa's left side. Reporters are surrounding them.

Generals Cesáreo Castro, Salvador Mercado, and Hernandez met. Their followers are in the background.

Sharpshooters were prepared to shower the city with their weapons, either from the hills or in street fighting. The smelter is in the background on the right in this well-organized photograph.

The federal forces used field artillery. This weapon is classified as a dynamite gun. This type of gun was used in the late 19th and early 20th centuries. It used compressed air to force the projectile through the barrel of the gun at a more measured rate. Early explosives could not be shot easily because of their unstable composition. They often blew up in the barrel of the weapon. When perfected, explosive shells replaced the dynamite gun.

Both federal forces and *insurrectos* had camp followers, many of whom were family members who cooked for the soldiers.

Trains brought many factions to Juárez. Here the Constitutionalists gathered at the trains after their arrival.

Many women supported the revolution. In this photograph, a group posed, some with their weapons and artillery belts. American women were among those who supported the goals of the revolution.

Americans, as well as soldiers of fortune from many places, gathered for the revolution. Among those well-known people are Sam Dreben, Tracy Richardson, and John Reed. There were many whose names will never be known, however. Jimmy Hare wrote letters to the editor of *Collier's* magazine that talked about the large number of Americans fighting for the *insurrectos*.

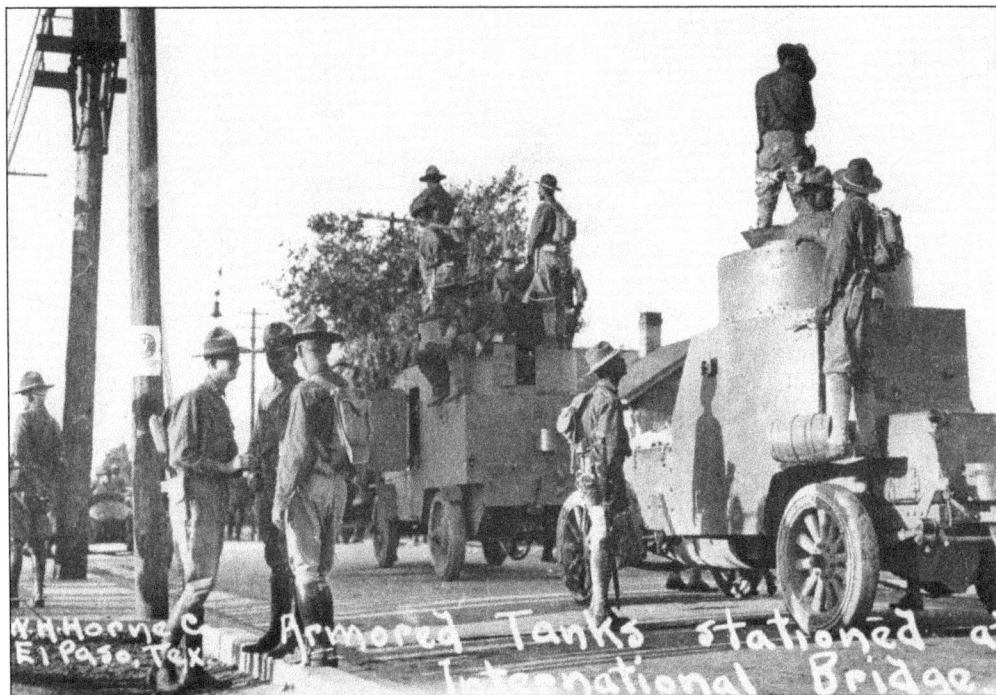

On the American side of the International Bridge, troops constantly manned the area of the customs house throughout the revolutionary period. There was a camp on the banks of the Rio Grande.

Intense fighting in Mexico caused armored tanks to be brought to the bridge.

This photograph shows a section of Chihuahuita, the bridge, and the banks of the river. Note the number of houses that are built right on the edge of the Rio Grande. The military encampment was to the left of the bridge and was also on the edge of the river.

Prior to the battle, various leaders gathered at Madero's camp to discuss their plans.

The Battle of Juárez began early on May 8, 1911. It lasted for four days. There was much destruction and death. Executions were common. Dead bodies littered the streets. This photograph shows a platoon of *insurrectos* going through the city.

Adobe was quite good protection. Soldiers used it when attacking and advancing their positions. Some soldiers of this group were already dead, but their comrades fought on.

After the battle, there was much destruction. Neighborhoods and office buildings were gone. The American section was decimated.

In El Paso, the newspapers kept up with the fighting by the minute. In a given day, there were as many as nine special editions printed. Reporters would synthesize information given in previous editions. Otis A. Aultman, noted photographer, was with Scott Photo and Pathé News. He also kept a scrapbook that showed a wonderful humor regarding the Mexican Revolution. On one page of this scrapbook he put the headlines from both El Paso newspapers for all the special editions.

Many homes were destroyed.

The post office was burned within two hours of the beginning of the battle.

Some places were left in total ruins.

Even the streets were destroyed.

Stores were looted.

Pancho Villa met with his troops after the battle.

His forces finally left town to join with those of Huerta, south of Juárez.

Pascual Orozco arranged with El Paso doctor Ira Bush to set up a field hospital for the revolutionary forces. Orozco and Bush met on several occasions to set up plans.

The Red Cross was also on site to assist casualties of the battle. This group of nurses is meeting with Gen. Francisco Murguia, who is in the center.

Prominent El Pasoans carried the injured back over the International Bridge for treatment in El Paso. Among those helping was Richard Burges, whose El Paso home is now the location of the El Paso County Historical Society.

Military ambulances were used to transport the wounded.

Many bodies were left on the battlefield, however.

They were also in the streets. The exact number of people killed is not known. In El Paso, less than 10 were killed by stray bullets.

Dead Federal Soldier
After the Battle of Juarez
Alexander
Photo
145

Both sides suffered casualties. Federal troops and *insurrectos* are checking the lined up bodies of their commands.

Insurrectos and federals executed anyone who was deemed an enemy. This famous picture shows a triple execution in the city.

In another execution, the victims' hands and feet were tied prior to being shot.

Mass graves were common. The cemetery was located southwest of the city.

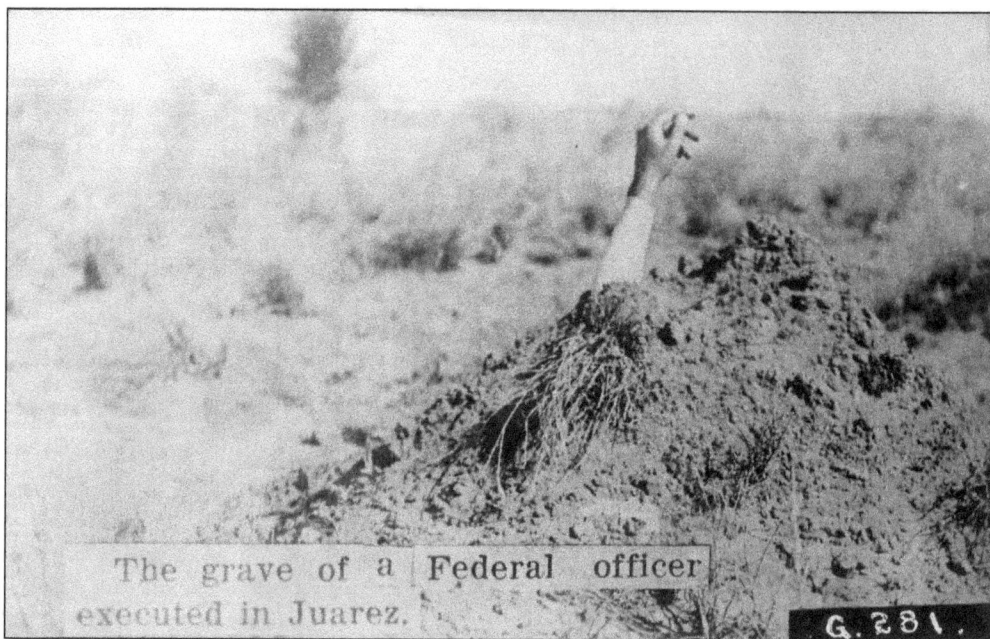

Some burials were simply hasty and not well done.

Orozco, Madero, and Garibaldi met after the battle. Madero claimed the presidency of Mexico. Orozco later fomented his own rebellion. Villa fired Garibaldi, who left the country for Europe.

Life went on in El Paso. Some people were put out by the disruption of their normal lives. One such person became engaged on the day of the Battle of Juárez. She and her new fiancé wanted to have lunch at their favorite restaurant in Juárez. They went, and she took some very good pictures immediately after the battle. She was not alone. The streets were crowded with souvenir hunters, and this was only two hours after the battle.

They ate lunch in their favorite restaurant, which had a hole in the wall and a cannonball on the floor near their table.

The Sunday following the battle, the streets were covered with sightseers. Many of the items they found have made their way to the museums and collections of today.

Five

THE YEARS BETWEEN
OJINAGA THROUGH COLUMBUS

After the Battle of Juárez, skirmishes and small battles occurred. There was also much strife within the revolutionary command. For some of the most significant events, only a few pictures were taken, most are of the aftermath.

They began in January 1914 with the Battle of Ojinaga, across the Rio Grande from Presidio, Texas. A long string of federal troops, their families, and Mexican citizens used this route out of Chihuahua to safety in the United States. A month later, "The Cumbre Tunnel Disaster" occurred. A train carrying 15 Americans among its passengers was robbed and the passengers then locked in their coach by Mexican bandits led by Maximo Castillo. A blazing freight train was sent into the tunnel from one direction, and the passenger train entered from the opposite side. The resulting collision and fire killed everyone.

In Washington, D.C., President Woodrow Wilson urged Americans to leave Mexico. After Díaz's fall, there was no protection for American business interests. In January 1916, the American staff at the CUSI Mining Company, owned by Potter Palmer Jr. and Honore Palmer of Chicago, was preparing to leave for El Paso and safety until the bandits roaming the countryside were subdued. The miners returned, but conditions were not good. They fled again. Bandits led by Pablo Lopez stopped their train at Santa Ysabel, Chihuahua. The Americans were taken off and executed. One person escaped, hid, and made his way back to El Paso to tell the tale. The town was furious. Anti-Mexican riots that the city was not able to control resulted. Fort Bliss troops led by Gen. John J. Pershing helped quell the disturbances.

Pancho Villa was furious at the United States for recognizing Venustiano Carranza as Mexico's president. Villa had been losing on the battlefield and in the eyes of the public because of banditry. He also needed weapons and ammunition. On March 9, 1916, his troops raided Columbus, New Mexico. A battle ensued, resulting in 17 Americans and over 100 Mexicans dead and much of the town of Columbus destroyed.

On Christmas Day 1917, bandits again struck the United States with a raid on Brite's Ranch in Presidio County, Texas, where several people were killed. Soldiers from Camp D. A. Russell and local citizens pursued the bandits and recovered much of what was stolen.

After the Battle of Juárez, there were other smaller battles. Small groups also roamed the countryside. These bandits raided ranches and towns. Retribution was sought. Common sights were people being hung from trees.

Executed bodies were also hung from telegraph poles.

Camps were established throughout the area from the Big Bend of Texas through New Mexico and into Arizona. In Texas, they went east of El Paso, following the line of Southern Pacific and Galveston, Harrisburg, and San Antonio Railroads. At Marfa, they went south to the Rio Grande. This camp was at Lajitas, Texas.

This remuda of horses was kept at the camp in Valentine, Texas.

The next significant battle was in Ojinaga, Mexico, in the winter of 1914. Pictures of the battle itself are not many. Mexican officers were on the border, as this postcard shows. (Courtesy Border Heritage Department, El Paso Public Library.)

The area is just outside what is today Big Bend National Park and across the river from Presidio, Texas. Other officers were also in the area. (Courtesy Border Heritage Department, El Paso Public Library.)

A leading *insurrecto* general was Salvador Mercado.

Federal forces were in Ojinaga, accompanied by refugees who were fleeing ahead of Villa's forces. Included in this group was Luis Terrazas, the wealthy landowner of Chihuahua. He had most of his family and money with him. The federal forces were defeated and escaped across the Rio Grande to the United States. Waiting on the American side were troops from Fort D. A. Russell in Marfa, Texas. They arrested the federal troops and marched them and the refugees to Marathon, Texas, in the January cold, where they boarded trains for internment at Fort Bliss, Texas. This particular picture depicts people crossing the river.

More Mexican nationals crossed with the troops. They waded the Rio Grande, which is not usually too high during the winter.

A federal ambulance brought wounded soldiers across the river.

Several people were placed into a single ambulance.

Family groups camped near the river before beginning the walk to Marathon.

Even the family dog was brought to safety.

Mex. refugee crossing the desert out at Ft. Bliss on way to camp

Everyone walked to Marathon. This was necessitated because there were not that many cars in the area at that time. Also, over 5,000 people crossed the river at the same time.

Some people were on horses, some were in wagons, others walked. All appear to have been dressed for the cold.

After boarding trains, the detainees were transported to Fort Bliss, Texas, where they were placed in a refugee camp. In this picture, the train is in the background and the refugees are beginning their walk to the internment camp.

It was a long procession, with the refugees watched by Fort Bliss personnel along the way.

The refugees were processed in tents and small buildings.

This took a long time.

At the beginning, fixing meals was an open-air process. It remained that way, but the preparation equipment for the meals improved over time.

The camp at Fort Bliss was set up with tents. Family units were together.

Adobe ovens were built outside individual tents.

Also, a typical kiva was made.

Everyone gathered for the celebration of Sunday mass.

Some camaraderie developed, such as this soldier and child saluting each other.

Casual lifestyles developed.

Berber shop in camp

A barber plied his trade in his federal officer's uniform.

The refugees from Ojinaga were not considered to be reliable with the violence that continued to happen on the border and in Juárez during the revolution. It was decided, therefore, to move them to Fort Wingate, New Mexico. Mexican Gen. Francisco Castro was in charge of the move. He and his family are pictured here as they prepare to board the train for Fort Wingate. Eventually the troops returned to Mexico. (Courtesy of Celia Berton.)

Bird's Eye View of Columbus N.M. 1226

By 1916, Madero had been assassinated and Huerta replaced by Venustiano Carranza. The U.S. government recognized Carranza, which enraged Pancho Villa. Villa had been suffering defeats and was short on ammunition, guns, and supplies. He had lost favor in El Paso because of the atrocities that had been committed after the battles of Juárez and Ojinaga. In the early morning hours of March 9, 1916, Villa invaded Columbus, New Mexico. The ensuing battle killed 17 soldiers and civilians. This is a picture of Columbus before the raid.

The Ruins of Columbus, N.M. after being Raided by Pancho Villa.

W.H. Horne Co. El Paso, Tex. 3017

After the raid, much of Columbus had been burned or destroyed.

American soldiers carry the coffins of soldiers killed at Columbus. (Courtesy Border Heritage Department, El Paso Public Library.)

The bodies of dead *insurrectos* were burned. Around 100 died.

This raid caused Woodrow Wilson to approve the Punitive Expedition into Mexico. Its purpose was to find and arrest Pancho Villa. The majority of the pictures of this raid can be found in *Somewhere in Mexico*, written by J. D. Givens. There are also many military photographs. Pictured here are some of Pershing's troops testing communications equipment.

The first use of American airplanes in a military setting was during the Punitive Expedition. The squadron was stationed at Columbus and covered the troops in Mexico. One of the planes is shown flying over the troops in 1916. (Courtesy of the Border Heritage Department of the El Paso Public Library.)

Troops remained at Camp Furlong in Columbus while others went into Mexico. Mexico was not happy with Wilson's decision to send troops there. Several meetings occurred regarding this subject.

During this time, Pablo Lopez was captured by Carranza's forces and executed, thus, ending the career of the man who orchestrated the massacre of American miners at Santa Ysabel.

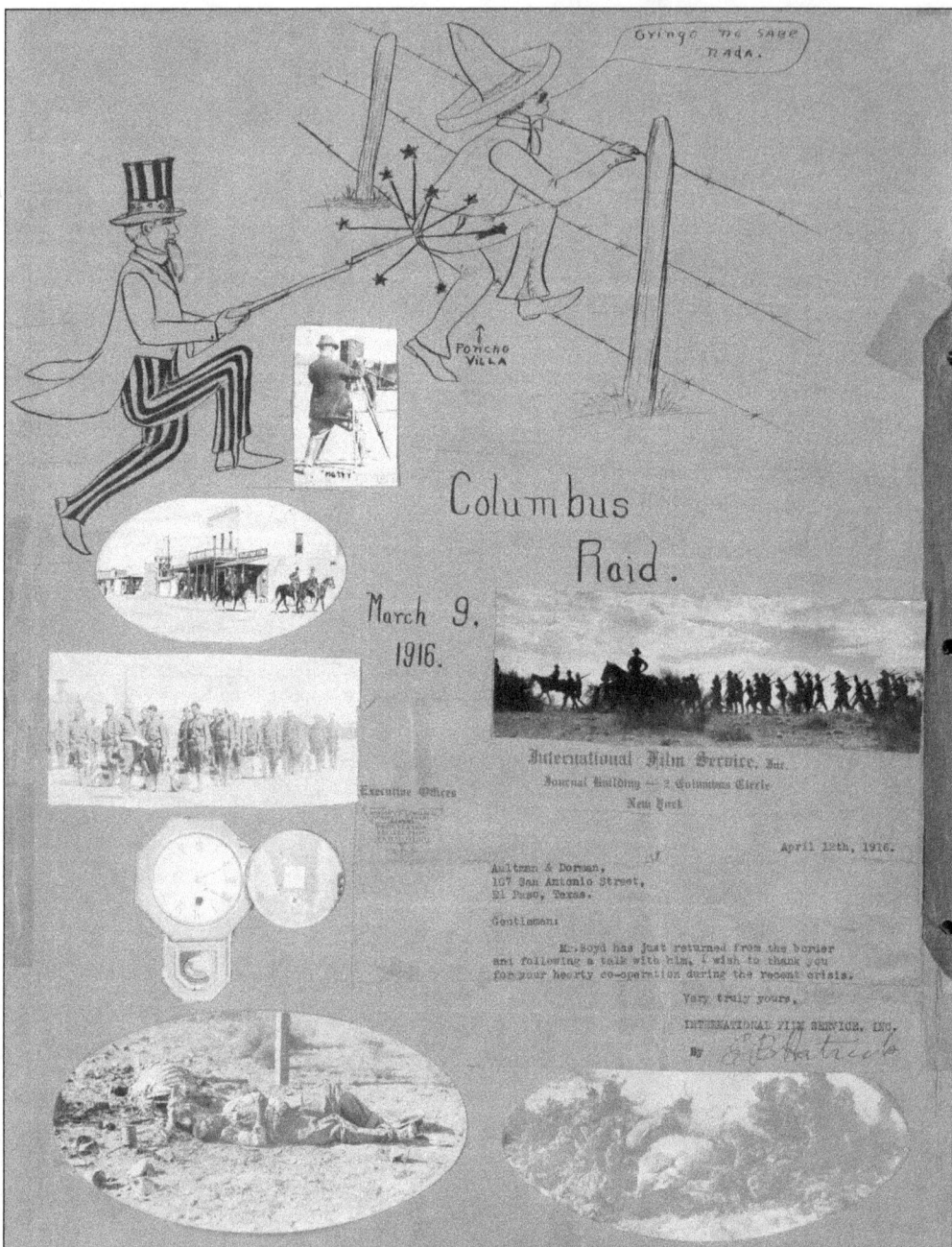

Otis Aultman went from El Paso to cover Columbus. This page is from his scrapbook and shows some of his humor. The film he took, as well as all other Aultman film, has disappeared as of this time. Some Columbus film made by an unidentified person is at the Library of Congress.

Six

FORT BLISS, THE MEXICAN REVOLUTION, AND EL PASO

Fort Bliss was established in El Paso in 1848. After being in several locations, the post moved to La Noria Mesa in 1898. It remains there and has expanded north, well into New Mexico, blending with White Sands Missile Range. Along the way it made El Paso an army town and a place known as being the "Mother-in-Law of the Army."

In 1909, troops participated in the Taft-Díaz visit, both in the parade and in protecting the presidents. As trouble in Mexico mounted, alertness increased at the post. At first it was more casual. Then, troops from all parts of the country were brought to the area to help with protection.

The gathering troops were assigned to camps set up all over town. They were Camps Baker, Beirne, Cotton, Pershing, Stewart, and Ysleta. There were some smaller units at Washington Park, Anapra, the cement plant (Camp Courchesne), Globe Mills, and the Santa Fe Street bridge. The majority of them were cavalry. The bridge camps were ready immediately after the revolution broke out. Troops were also waiting on the north side of the river after the Battle of Ojinaga. Fort Bliss, and then Fort Wingate, New Mexico, housed between 4,000 and 5,000 refugees from the Battle of Ojinaga. In total, approximately 100,000 troops served on the U.S. border with Mexico during the Mexican Revolution.

Gen. John J. Pershing became the commander of the post in April 1914. Gen. Hugh Scott was the southern military district commander. At the same time as the revolution, World War I was beginning. When Pershing arrived in El Paso, he wanted to impress the city's citizens with the knowledge that they were secure by showing the post's military might. There were several parades, one of which was 25 miles long. Fort Bliss provides basic training even today.

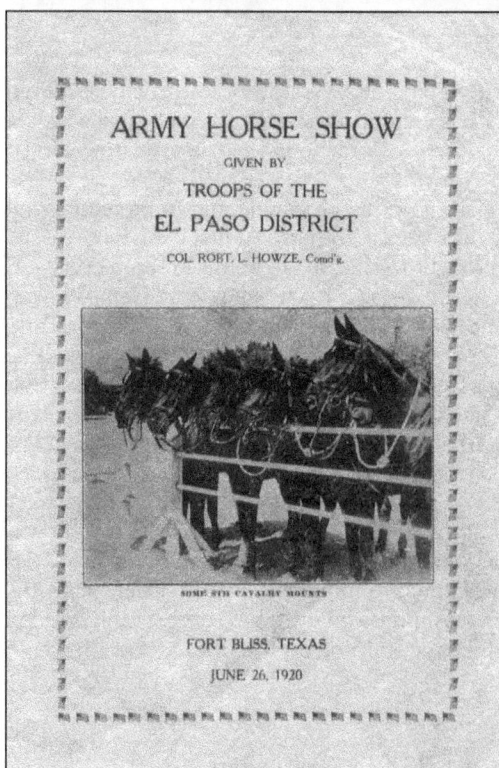

ARMY HORSE SHOW

GIVEN BY

TROOPS OF THE

EL PASO DISTRICT

COL. ROBT. L. HOWZE, Cond'g.

SOME 8TH CAVALRY MOUNTS

FORT BLISS, TEXAS

JUNE 26, 1920

Fort Bliss located to its present site in 1898. At the time, Officer's Row was built and a few smaller buildings were in place. One can see that in 1898, El Paso had beautiful native grasses that extended to the Hueco Mountains.

In the early years, Fort Bliss was an active cavalry post. Soldiers participated in and also hosted local races and horse shows.

When the Mexican Revolution began, the soldiers at the post were immediately on alert. The first place protected was the International Bridge.

As activity increased, National Guard and reserve units from across the United States were posted to the border to help defend it. Among them was Company M, 1st South Carolina Infantry.

Trucks were ready beside the various camps.

The Mexican Revolution era was also the beginning of the use of modern military equipment. Pictured is an early machine gun unit.

This armor-plated truck has left many wondering if it could move.

Camps were positioned all over town, with most concentrated along the border. The Ormsbee photograph albums provide numerous shots of units stationed relatively near the smelter. This group is the 8th Massachusetts Company in 1916. The smelter stacks are in the background.

Camp Stewart was on the eastern part of the city's border.

Camp Cotton was at the base of Cotton Street in central El Paso, near the Rio Grande.

Maneuvers were undertaken along the river.

Most soldiers lived in tents. This was Camp Courchesne.

Soldiers often participated in parades that celebrated both the military and city events. This parade occurred June 7, 1916.

Mayor Tom Lea Jr. joined General Bell leading one parade.

Ohio artillery in 20 mi. parade

When Gen. John Pershing became commander of Fort Bliss, he wanted to show that the post was ready to support and protect El Paso. Troops participated in all parades, including the famous 25-mile parade (identified here as a 20-mile parade). The Ohio artillery was part of that event.

In 1916, World War I had broken out in Europe, and troops marched in the city's preparedness parade.

Among the most impressive parades were those where the cavalry units lined the streets in honor of the units passing.

Thanksgiving on the Border

One day each year is set aside,
No matter where you're living,
You always get a nice large feed;
We call this day Thanksgiving.

We're a bunch of jolly fellows
Camped here on the border line,
And for a better dinner
You may look, but never find.

There is everything before you,
Just like you were at home;
So let us all be thankful,
Don't let your memories roam.

No one knows of the future,
As we're gathered here today,
And our next Thanksgiving dinner
May be many miles away.

When the call to colors sounded
We all held up our hand,
And left our homes and sweethearts
For a cause most good and grand.

At Camp Baker we are training,
For the fray across the sea,
And when we leave for Sunny France,
A happy bunch we'll be.

We've trained hard here in Texas,
In the wind storm and the sand,
And built some fifty bridges,
Across the Rio Grande.

It's Uncle Sam we're serving,
And each and every one
Must do his best at every test,
And we're bound to beat the Hun.

But as this is Thanksgiving,
We'll forget the gun and sword,
And bow our heads in reverend prayer,
Let's give thanks to our Lord.

—G. J. S.

Various camps at the post celebrated holidays with official programs. A soldier known only by his initials wrote this poem that appeared in the Camp Baker Thanksgiving menu program. The unit was training to go to war in Europe.

The Punitive Expedition did not find Pancho Villa. In 1919, Villa amassed another group of soldiers and once again attacked Juárez. Sharpshooters fired on El Paso, injuring several people. 3,600 American soldiers were ordered to cross into Mexico to fight Villa. The 24th Infantry Regiment, 5th Cavalry, 7th Cavalry, and 2nd Battalion, 82nd FA entered Juárez. They destroyed Villa's force of 1,200 at the Bull Ring. Villa escaped. Some of the soldiers are shown returning over the International Bridge.

Villa was assassinated in 1923. Active rebellions ceased until 1929, when Gen. José Gonzalo Escobar mounted another revolution. Escobar planned to force the United States to recognize his presidency by assuming office at the exact time when the American presidency was transferred from one president to another, in this case from Calvin Coolidge to Herbert Hoover. It would force the United States to accept the Escobar presidency by default. The plan failed; Escobar fled Mexico.

A machine gun battery was captured from Escobar supporters.

The military presence on the border was recognized nationally. Shown is a Bull Durham advertisement from *Popular Science Monthly*. Two soldiers at Camp Cotton are enjoying their tobacco. There is no date on the advertisement.

Seven

WHO COVERED THIS REVOLUTION?

In the early 20th century, moving pictures were just beginning. The cameras were primitive. They received their first field trials during the Mexican Revolution. The film at the time was silver nitrate—not much of which remains today. In El Paso, Otis Aultman was the first to use film extensively. In a 1920 edition of an El Paso Chamber of Commerce publication, Aultman listed the film he had done for Pathé News. None of it has been located.

The medium of choice during the revolution was a picture that was then processed to a postcard. These are known as real-picture postcards. Numerous photographers took many stills. The best of the photographs wound up on postcards. Vast numbers of them remain. There are collections all over the United States and Mexico. Most are related to individual photographers. They can be found at The University of Texas at Austin, Texas A & M University, Yale University, The University of Texas at El Paso, Texas Tech University, Sul Ross State University, and the El Paso Public Library, to name a few. The great Casasola collection is in Mexico.

At the El Paso County Historical Society, several collections, contemporary to the time, were donated over the years. Those are featured in this book. Among the photographers represented are Jim A. Alexander, W. H. Horne, Otis A. Aultman, D. W. Hoffman, Jimmy Hare, and Fred Feldman. Feldman was an excellent portrait photographer. All of them followed the battles and any activities in the city. Lately, material has been surfacing at local estate sales. The amateur photographer got some shots the professional would not have done, and they are just as interesting and definitely more personal.

By far, the largest remaining photograph collection in El Paso is that of Otis A. Aultman. The photographs are officially at the El Paso Public Library. There are many copies. His scrapbook at the El Paso County Historical Society is most interesting, and it is only 19 pages. Aultman is shown filming during the revolution.

Aultman lived in the studio whose darkroom is shown here. There was a loft over one area, and that is where he lived. Unfortunately, in 1947, he fell out of the loft, broke his neck, and died. (Courtesy of the Border Heritage Department of the El Paso Public Library.)

Reporters gathered in this photograph of one unknown person, two by last name only, and one, Jimmy Hare, exceptionally well known. Hare's photographs are considered to be some of the very best of the Mexican Revolution. Even the consul's wife praised them. It is possible that the Scott in this picture was the owner of Scott Photographic Studio, where Aultman worked.

Aultman (right) is playing cards with an unidentified person. (Courtesy of the Otis A. Aultman Collection, Border Heritage Department of the El Paso Public Library.)

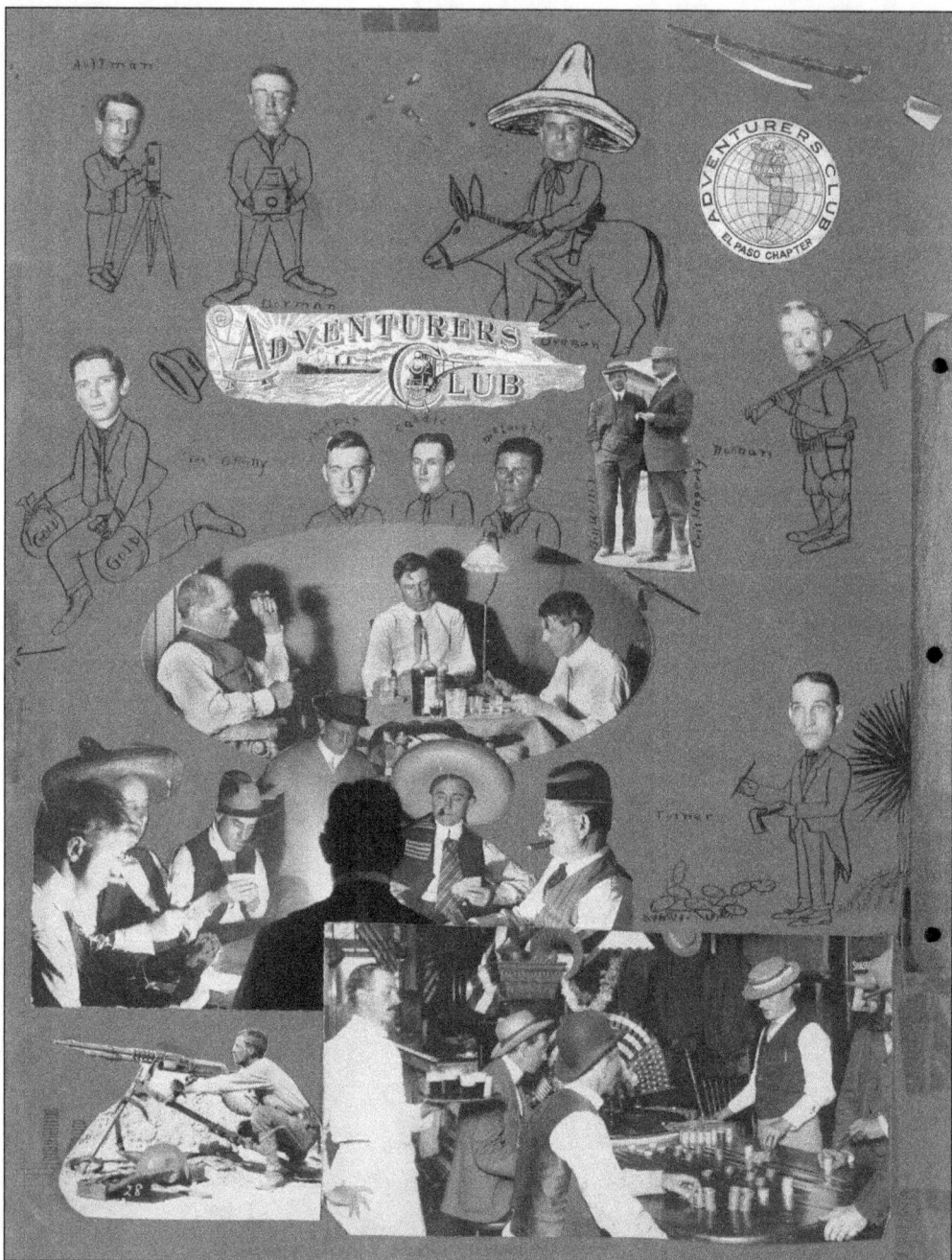

One of the area's more interesting groups was the Adventurer's Club that met in Aultman's studio. They played cards and drank. Among the more famous members of this group were Tracy Richardson and Sam Dreben. Aultman devoted a page of his scrapbook to the Adventurer's Club.

The Mutual Film Company brought their photographers and film crew by train. Among their group was John Reed, who went to the Russian Revolution after Mexico. The Museum of Big Bend Studies in Alpine, Texas, has a copy of their film. (Courtesy of the Otis A. Aultman Collection, Border Heritage Department of the El Paso Public Library.)

Charles Pryor was the owner of the El Paso Feature Film Company. He filmed the Battle of Ojinaga in what is some of the earliest battle film. The film from this battle is at the Library of Congress. Depicted is the leadership of the *insurrectos* in staged poses. For some, it was their last battle. Pryor created this poster for publicity. It is quite colorful. He wound up in prison in California. This story has been featured on *History Detectives* on PBS.

Postcards were the printing method of choice during the Mexican Revolution. W. H. Horne had a shop in South El Paso where he produced them. In this photograph, the store on the right advertises postcards for sale. (Courtesy of the C. L. Sonnichsen Special Collections Department, the Library, The University of Texas at El Paso.)

James A. Alexander is a mystery photographer of the Mexican Revolution. His photographic career in El Paso began near the Aultman studio on El Paso Street and concluded in the 1920s with offices on Alameda. For several years after the Mexican Revolution, he continued to sell prints. He is responsible for most of the pictures of the internment camp at Fort Bliss. Alexander also had an office in Cloudcroft, New Mexico, and took many pictures of the Sacramento Mountains. One of his works is this nicely composed picture of Hotel Dieu Hospital.

The press gathered in mass on the steps of the courthouse for Victoriano Huerta's trial. (Courtesy of the Otis A. Aultman Collection, Border Heritage Department of the El Paso Public Library.)

On the Roof Garden of Hotel Paso del Norte. The only Hotel in the World offering its Guests a Safe, Comfortable Place to View a Mexican Revolution

One of the most used postcards from the Mexican Revolution era is the famous picture of newsmen standing on the roof of the Paso del Norte. Its statement of being a safe place to watch a Mexican Revolution does not apply to 1911, for which this card has been used many times. It is from the final revolution of the period, Escobar's in 1929.

BIBLIOGRAPHY

American Institute of Mining Engineers. *Transactions of the American Institute of Mining Engineers, Vol. XXXII*. New York, NY: The Institute, 1902.

Atkin, Ronald, *Revolution! Mexico 1910–20*. New York, NY: The John Day Company, 1970.

Border Heritage Department, El Paso Public Library, El Paso, TX.

Bush, I. J. *Gringo Doctor*. Caldwell, Idaho: The Caxton Printers, Ltd., 1939.

The C. L. Sonnichsen Special Collections Department, Library, The University of Texas at El Paso. El Paso, TX: The Mexican Revolution Collection.

El Paso County Historical Society, Mexican Revolution Collections. El Paso, TX.

Habermeyer, Christopher Lance. *Gringos' Curve, Pancho Villa's Massacre of American Miners in Mexico, 1916*. El Paso, TX: Christopher Lance Habermeyer, 2004.

Harris III, Charles H. and Louis R. Sadler. *The Secret War in El Paso: Mexican Revolutionary Intrigue, 1906–1920*. Albuquerque, NM: University of New Mexico Press, 2009.

Keith, Noel L. *The Brites of Capote*. Fort Worth, TX: Texas Christian University Press, 1950.

Metz, Leon. *Fort Bliss, An Illustrated History*. El Paso, TX: Mangan Books, 1981.

———. *El Paso Chronicles*. El Paso, TX: Mangan Books, 1993.

Morales, Fred. *El Paso and Juárez During the Mexican Revolution. Volume I, 1879–1911*. El Paso, TX: Fred Morales, 2010.

Romo, David Dorado. *Ringside Seat to a Revolution*. El Paso, TX: Cinco Puntas Press, 2005.

Siller, Pedro and Miguel Ángel Berumen. *La Batal de Ciudad Juárez, I. La Historia; II. Las Imagenes*. Ciudad Juárez, Mexico: Cuadro por Cuadro, 2003.

Sonnichsen, C. L. *Pass of the North, Four Centuries on the Rio Grande*. El Paso, TX: Texas Western Press, 1990.

Timmons, W. H. *El Paso, A Borderlands History*. El Paso, TX: Texas Western Press, 1990.

Vanderwood, Paul J. and Frank N. Samponaro. *Border Fury, A Picture Postcard Record of Mexico's Revolution and U.S. War Preparedness, 1910–1917*. Albuquerque, NM: University of New Mexico Press, 1988.

EL PASO COUNTY HISTORICAL SOCIETY

The El Paso County Historical Society, a nonprofit 501(c)(3) organization, was chartered February 17, 1955. The primary objectives of the society are "to foster research into the history of the El Paso area; to acquire and make available to the public historical materials; to publish and encourage historical writing pertaining to the area and to develop public consciousness of our rich historical heritage."

For many years, the Pioneer Association kept track of the early archives of El Paso. When the Historical Society was created, those accumulated records formed the basis for its collections. Other donations over the years increased the size of its archival holdings. In addition to the Pioneer Association materials, the society has particularly strong collections of photographs, postcards, scrapbooks, and documents including those from the Daughters of the Confederacy and El Paso Natural Gas. Other items are added regularly.

The El Paso County Historical Society is the largest local historical society in Texas, with over 700 members. It publishes *Password*, an academic journal, and *El Conquistador*, a newsletter, on a quarterly basis. There are quarterly meetings open to all. Each year it hosts the Hall of Honor in which one living and up to two deceased El Pasoans who have made a significant contribution to the city's history are honored. It participates in Tom Lea month and, in the spring, hosts Dollie Dingle's Tea Party.

The society is an all-volunteer organization that is open three days each week. Other times can be arranged. It is located at 603 West Yandell, El Paso, Texas 79902. New members are always welcome. You can click the "join now" statement online at www.elpasohistory.com, and an application will be mailed to you.

Visit us at
arcadiapublishing.com

....

www.ingramcontent.com/pod-product-compliance
Lightning Source LLC
Chambersburg PA
CBHW080626110426
42813CB00006B/1612